CAPTAIN
Sir Tom Moore
ONE HUNDRED STEPS

Illustrated by
Adam Larkum

PUFFIN

*O*N A BRIGHT APRIL MORNING, a ninety-nine-year-old man stood outside his house and held on to his walking frame. His name was Captain Tom Moore, and he had pledged to walk one hundred lengths of his garden in time for his one hundredth birthday, to raise money for the doctors and nurses risking their lives to save others.

Tom took a deep breath. He knew this wasn't going to be easy. But he told himself one of the many important things he'd learnt during his long life . . .

The first step is always the hardest,
but unless you take that first step,
you'll never finish.

Tom grew up in a small town called Keighley, in Yorkshire.
His dad built houses, and his mum was a teacher.

Even though most boys avoided the kitchen in those days, Tom loved spending hours cooking with his mum. Enormous cakes with coloured icing, thick-crusted pies, and fancy three-course meals. She taught him that it didn't matter who you were . . .

You can do and be
anything you want.

When he wasn't in the kitchen, Tom was outside playing with his dog, Billy. They went everywhere together on adventures in the garden and exploring the town, but best of all they loved running, wild and free, on the Yorkshire moors.

Billy was named after Tom's favourite uncle, who raced motorbikes, and taught Tom how to ride. At night, Tom would lie in bed remembering the roar of the engine and the feeling of freedom he felt as the wheels spun beneath him. *One day*, he said to himself, *I'll have a motorbike of my very own.*

Tom worked hard at school. In lessons he was quiet and well behaved, and he got on with his teachers and classmates.

But he wasn't above bending the rules. When he was twelve, Tom bought his first motorbike and he rode it everywhere he could – he would even hide it in the school grounds so that he could look at it at lunchtime!

And Tom's motorbike wasn't the only thing he would sneak into school . . .

As Tom grew older, he spent more and more time riding his motorbike. He and Billy would spend whole days racing across the moors, grinning ear to ear as the wind whipped through their hair and the sun bounced brightly off the motorbike.

Every day can be an adventure!

In 1939, when Tom was nineteen, war was declared. It was a worrying time but Tom wanted to serve his country, and so the next year he signed up as an officer in the army. Seagulls wheeled overhead as he waved goodbye to his family to go far away to fight.

Tom's ship was bound for a country called
Burma, in South-east Asia. It made
many stops along the way – from the
bustling, dusty harbour in Freetown,
the capital city of Sierra Leone . . .

. . . to the awe-inspiring
Table Mountain in
Cape Town, South Africa.

It took many weeks to reach
Burma and Tom would never
forget the people he met or
the incredible things he saw
throughout the journey.

Life in Burma took some getting used to – especially the enormous bugs and creepy-crawlies that lived in the jungle, including a spider as big as Tom's hand! Tom made use of his love of engines, and his talent for fixing things, by teaching the troops how to ride and fix motorbikes – and then tanks.

War could be scary, and Tom missed his family, but he and his new friends made sure to have fun, too. They would take holidays around the country and even travelled to try to see Mount Everest, the tallest mountain in the world – but it was cloudy, so all they could see was fog.

And on special occasions there were parties and concerts – once, the famous singer Vera Lynn made the long journey from Britain to visit the troops and to sing for them. Tom could hardly believe that he was seeing her with his own eyes!

I know we'll meet again some sunny day.

So, even though Tom, along with the rest of the world, was pleased when the war finally ended and he could go home, he missed his friends and the amazing sights he had seen.

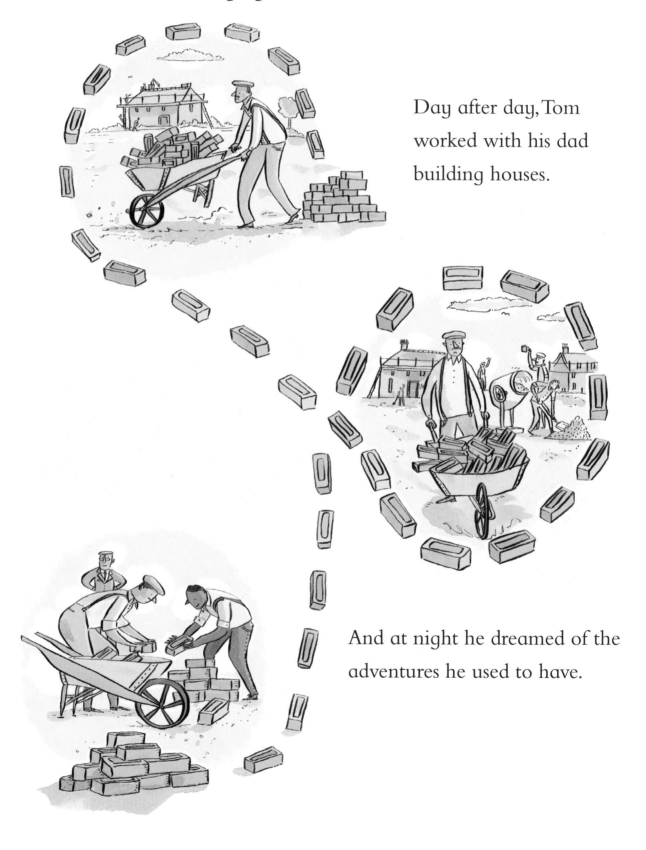

Day after day, Tom worked with his dad building houses.

And at night he dreamed of the adventures he used to have.

Tom wasn't ready to give up on adventure though, and he rediscovered the wonderful feeling of freedom that he had always found riding motorbikes. He started to race in events called time trials and he won race after race after race! Tom knew then that even when the sky seems full of dark grey clouds . . .

The Sun will Shine again.

And the greatest adventure of Tom's life began when he met Pamela. He thought she was the most beautiful person he'd ever seen and made excuses to travel the great distance between their home towns to see her.

Before long, they fell deeply in love.

After Tom and Pamela got married, they had two little girls –
Lucy and Hannah. They taught the girls about cooking
and about fixing engines.

Hannah was the smallest,
so her job was to change
the oil in the car!

Tom had never forgotten
the lesson his mother had
taught him. No matter
who you are . . .

You can do and be anything you want.

As the years went by, Tom and Pamela's family grew
and grew
and grew!

Lucy and Hannah had
children of their own . . .

Tom   Pamela   Lucy   Tom   Hannah   Colin

Benjie

Georgia

Harry   Thomas   Max   Charlie

and there were always new dogs!

Over the years, Tom made sure that
the family had lots of adventures, and their days
were filled with laughter and mischief –
and the dogs made more mischief than anyone!

But sadly, when Pamela was sixty-three years old,
she got sick and, eight years later, she passed away.

Without Pamela, Tom was very, very sad. But he surrounded himself with his family and they helped him to find happy days again. In fact, these years were the happiest of his life so far. His family showed Tom that . . .

At the end of the storm, there is a golden sky.

They certainly kept him busy fixing things.

He kept an eye on the garden, even though
things didn't always go to plan.

And he made sure to go off for the odd adventure . . .

... like travelling to Everest, so that he could finally see it with his own eyes! It was a very long journey for a ninety-year-old and Tom could hardly believe it when he saw Everest at last, the mountain rising, bold and majestic, ahead of him. It took his breath away.

It's never too late
for one more
adventure.

So, when a dangerous disease swept around the world,
Tom knew that he had to do something to help others,
just as his family had helped him.

Together they had the idea . . .

. . . to raise money
by walking one hundred lengths of his garden,
in time for his one hundredth birthday.

Every day, Tom went out into the garden and,
slowly but surely, walked step after step after step.
And before he knew it . . .

...the whole world was watching him!

Because one step has the power

to inspire one hundred more!

Tom couldn't believe how many cards arrived for his
one hundredth birthday! As he read the outpourings of love
and admiration, he thought about all the people who had
written to him, and what he would like to say in reply:

For all those finding it difficult: the sun will shine
on you again and the clouds will go away.
Remember that tomorrow will be a good day.

About Captain Sir Tom Moore

CAPTAIN SIR TOM MOORE was born in Keighley, in the West Riding of Yorkshire, in April 1920. Over the course of his long life he has seen and done some extraordinary things – too many to fit in just one book!

The world has changed a lot since Tom was born. When he was a little boy, his father bought the first car in their street – at the time, everything was delivered by horse-drawn cart.

That car must have inspired Tom in his lifelong love of engines and fixing things. When he was twelve years old, he found a motorbike in a barn and bought it for half a crown. (In today's money, that's about £9!)

Tom enlisted as an officer in the army in the Second World War and served in the Royal Armoured Corps in India and Burma. During the war, he saw many incredible things, including monkeys, snakes, and spiders the size of his hand! Once the war was over, he flew all the way home from India in a Sunderland flying boat, via Bahrain, Egypt and Italy before he landed in Poole Harbour.

After the war, Tom took part in motorbike time trials and drove a three-wheeler red sports car. He was one of the very first people to drive on the first motorway in Britain, soon after it opened, in 1959.

As a boy, with his mother and sister

As an officer in the army

Riding his motorbike

Captain Sir Tom Moore walking for the NHS in 2020

During the coronavirus pandemic in 2020, Tom inspired the nation by walking one hundred laps of his garden in time for his one hundredth birthday, raising nearly £40 million for charity and providing a voice of hope during a dark time. In recognition of his incredible work, he was awarded an honorary promotion to colonel, a knighthood and a gold Blue Peter Badge!

With thanks to Captain Sir Tom Moore,
Hannah Ingram-Moore, Colin Ingram-Moore,
Benjie Ingram-Moore, Georgia Ingram-Moore,
Lucy Teixeira, Tom Teixeira, Tom Teixeira, Max Teixeira,
Adam Larkum, Bev James, Megan Carver,
Anna Barnes Robinson and Keren-Orr Greenfeld

The Captain Tom Foundation was created in response to the most amazing love and support
given to Captain Sir Tom and his family, not only from the Great British Public
but around the world, in response to Tom's Walk 100 for the NHS.
The family wanted to create a lasting legacy – the mission:
To Inspire Hope where it is Needed Most
We have identified causes close to our hearts:
Combating loneliness
Helping those facing bereavement
Supporting hospices

https://captaintom.org

PUFFIN BOOKS

UK | USA | Canada | Ireland | Australia | India | New Zealand | South Africa

Puffin Books is part of the Penguin Random House group of companies
whose addresses can be found at global.penguinrandomhouse.com.

www.penguin.co.uk   www.puffin.co.uk   www.ladybird.co.uk

Penguin
Random House
UK

First published 2020
006

Text copyright © Tom Moore, 2020
Illustrations copyright © Adam Larkum, 2020

'We'll Meet Again' lyrics by Hughie Charles and Ross Parker; © Music Sales Corp., 1939

The moral right of the author and illustrator has been asserted

Printed in Italy

A CIP catalogue record for this book is available from the British Library

ISBN: 978–0–241–48676–4

All correspondence to: Puffin Books, Penguin Random House Children's
One Embassy Gardens, 8 Viaduct Gardens, London SW11 7BW